in case of emergency press

We are proud to acknowledge the Traditional Owners of country throughout Australia and to recognise their continuing connection to land, waters, and culture.

We pay our respects to their Elders:
past, present, and emerging.

We support recognition, reconciliation, and reparation.

Finishing Stroke

Poems

Peter Murphy

in case of emergency press

http://www.icoe.com.au
Travancore, Victoria
Australia

Published by **in case of emergency press** 2021

Copyright © Peter Murphy 2021

All rights reserved. Without limiting the rights under copyright reserved above, no part of this publication may be reproduced, stored in or introduced into a database and retrieval system or transmitted in any form or any means (electronic, mechanical, photocopying, recording or otherwise) without the prior written permission of both the owner of copyright and the above publishers.

ISBN 978-0-6451280-1-7

Acknowledgements

Poems in this book have appeared in the following publications;

Polestar Writers' Journal, unusual work, The Mozzie, Poetry Matters, Overland, The Attitude of Cups, The Age, Short and Twisted, Sidewalk, Centoria, fine line, Arena, The Best Australian Poems 2012, Mixed Concrete Poetry, Poetry for Public Transport, Gangway, Quadrant, The Quadrant Book of Poetry 2001 – 2010, Writers' Radio, Thirst, Meanjin, 'r', La Trobe Forum.

What can you edit out
without losing
everything?

from 'The Right Notes'

Table of contents

Nice of the French	1
For the Slow Reader	2
Mausoleum at Charlottenburg	3
The Beechworth Mental Hospital	4
Actor	5
highlights	7
Haiku (1)	8
indistinguishable	9
Bee on Arrival	10
Gardening	11
end of the line	12
A Detective Calls	13
'MANIAR'	14
foreign	15
Don't/let yourself go	16
Conversations	17
The Detective	18
Loop: At The Kaiservilla	19
life afterlife	20
Haiku (2)	21
TV People	22
Slips of the Tongue	23
'Hanged'	25
Lost in the Emporium	26
No need to fuss	28
Haiku (3)	29
When the first knight	30
Homage to the Arts of Empire	31
Celebration Day	33
Appearances	34
Afterwards	35
No one sits down	36
Just as the radio guru	37

Dracula Comes Home	38
SOMETHING	40
Horrible	41
Haiku (4)	42
Behind the Window	43
Cloud of Forgetfulness #3	44
Possessions	45
Virtual Germany	46
Who is George Clooney?	47
People Begging	48
Correction	49
Somewhere/in the growth	50
The Machine Jars	51
Movie	52
It's the faces in the background	53
The Albums	54
SUUBLIME	55
Icon	56
Sedative Ad	57
The Tourist's Fear of Missing Something	59
Autopsy Shows	60
Goodbye Tiny Tim	61
Running Back	62
101 Dalmatians	63
Haiku (5)	64
Always Eating	65
Bench	66
I remember her last call	67
Entering	68
minimum	69
Fox	70
Whether across the sky	71
Wings of Angels	72
The Blank Page	73
Haiku (6)	74

Finishing Stroke

Grand Prix	75
Cursor	76
What becomes of the Queen's hats?	77
That Face	78
Europe and Almonds	79
Haiku (7)	80
Bodies on TV	81
Powerful Friends	83
'FREE DUBCEK'	84
Friday Night in the Supermarket	85
Boredom	86
Gerry's Bag	87
Desktop Diary	88
Haiku (8)	89
Jottings in the Margin	90
There's something about the suburbs	91
The owner walks the dog	92
Venice	93
ANTARCTICA	95
Haiku (9)	96
Green	97
Because celluloid preserves flesh	98
Terms and Conditions	99
an old handmower	100
dead over fifty years	101
after a long sermon	102
Peoples permanently at war	103
plus minus	104
The Right Notes	105
For the slow	106
What to do Next	107
Person or Persons Unknown	108
Footnotes	110
in/ the/ full/ness	111
2022	112
About the Author	113

Finishing Stroke

Poems

Peter Murphy

nice
of the French
to term
the finishing
stroke the
coup de grâce

grace
being one

of those many
open-ended
words

For the Slow Reader

the history of the world moves
very slowly.
Fiction takes forever

in reaching its climaxes: the next line
is always coming and
explanations

take so long
early steps are forgotten.

Chapters start to inconclusively
drag around the middle,
the beginning a haze, the end

unreachable.

Mausoleum at Charlottenburg

This gorgeous palace, once serving to display
the power and wealth of the Hohenzollerns,
has become a theme park
so popular with tourists
the guide book warns about weekends.

Our combined ticket takes us through
the upper floor of the Old Palace
and the Mausoleum
—which looks more
glamorously sinister
than anything—

dark, elegant, classical
at the end of a path,
large trees
disguising the entrance.

At the desk, while
our ticket is punched
we say
how cool it is
wondering

whether those within
realized the price of grandeur
was endless
display.

The Beechworth Mental Hospital

Formerly an asylum
then the mental hospital
now a park/historic site

still with the old, deceptive wall
low on the outside
the locals never meant to know
it's twice as high inside

the ground in there
(cut away at the base)
tapering up a gentle hill
to the smooth lawn near
the water garden.

Outsiders might never guess
you were desperate
to leave.

Actor

At an exhibition of horror movie props
I encountered an actor
dressed as Dracula.

The flyer said
he'd be in his casket
or on the move.

In my first three passes
I saw the casket's
red satin padding
but not him

and thought he might've
knocked off

and then he was coming towards me
without expression

slowly
with perfect composure
as if in some other
reality

and I looked to him
for some kind of recognition
or acknowledgment of his role

and mine

but he kept coming at me
without expression
as if he really were
what he appeared to be

as with an uneasy
thrill
I moved away to let him
(but which

'him'?)

pass.

```
hhhhhhhhhhhhhhhhhhhhhhhhhhhhhhhhhhhhhhhhhhhhhhhhhhhhhhhhhhhhhhhhhhhhhhhhhh
iiiiiiiiiiiiiiiiiiiiiiiiiiiiiiiiiiiiiiiiiiiiiiiiiiiiiiiiiiiiiiiiiiiiiiiiii
gggggggggggggggggggggggggggggggggggggggggggggggggggggggggggggggggggggggggg
hhhhhhhhhhhhhhhhhhhhhhhhhhhhhhhhhhhhhhhhhhhhhhhhhhhhhhhhhhhhhhhhhhhhhhhhhh
llllllllllllllllllllllllllllllllllllllllllllllllllllllllllllllllllllllllll
iiiiiiiiiiiiiiiiiiiiiiiiiiiiiiiiiiiiiiiiiiiiiiiiiiiiiiiiiiiiiiiiiiiiiiiiii
gggggggggggggggggggggggggggggggggggggggggggggggggggggggggggggggggggggggggg
hhhhhhhhhhhhhhhhhhhhhhhhhhhhhhhhhhhhhhhhhhhhhhhhhhhhhhhhhhhhhhhhhhhhhhhhhh
tttttttttttttttttttttttttttttttttttttttttttttttttttttttttttttttttttttttttt
ssssssssssssssssssssssssssssssssssssssssssssssssssssssssssssssssssssssssss
hhhhhhhhhhhhhhhhhhhhhhhhhhhhhhhhhhhhhhhhhhhhhhhhhhhhhhhhhhhhhhhhhhhhhhhhhh
iiiiiiiiiiiiiiiiiiiiiiiiiiiiiiiiiiiiiiiiiiiiiiiiiiiiiiiiiiiiiiiiiiiiiiiiii
gggggggggggggggggggggggggggggggggggggggggggggggggggggggggggggggggggggggggg
hhhhhhhhhhhhhhhhhhhhhhhhhhhhhhhhhhhhhhhhhhhhhhhhhhhhhhhhhhhhhhhhhhhhhhhhhh
llllllllllllllllllllllllllllllllllllllllllllllllllllllllllllllllllllllllll
iiiiiiiiiiiiiiiiiiiiiiiiiiiiiiiiiiiiiiiiiiiiiiiiiiiiiiiiiiiiiiiiiiiiiiiiii
gggggggggggggggggggggggggggggggggggggggggggggggggggggggggggggggggggggggggg
hhhhhhhhhhhhhhhhhhhhhhhhhhhhhhhhhhhhhhhhhhhhhhhhhhhhhhhhhhhhhhhhhhhhhhhhhh
tttttttttttttttttttttttttttttttttttttttttttttttttttttttttttttttttttttttttt
ssssssssssssssssssssssssssssssssssssssssssssssssssssssssssssssssssssssssss
hhhhhhhhhhhhhhhhhhhhhhhhhhhhhhhhhhhhhhhhhhhhhhhhhhhhhhhhhhhhhhhhhhhhhhhhhh
iiiiiiiiiiiiiiiiiiiiiiiiiiiiiiiiiiiiiiiiiiiiiiiiiiiiiiiiiiiiiiiiiiiiiiiiii
gggggggggggggggggggggggggggggggggggggggggggggggggggggggggggggggggggggggggg
hhhhhhhhhhhhhhhhhhhhhhhhhhhhhhhhhhhhhhhhhhhhhhhhhhhhhhhhhhhhhhhhhhhhhhhhhh
llllllllllllllllllllllllllllllllllllllllllllllllllllllllllllllllllllllllll
iiiiiiiiiiiiiiiiiiiiiiiiiiiiiiiiiiiiiiiiiiiiiiiiiiiiiiiiiiiiiiiiiiiiiiiiii
gggggggggggggggggggggggggggggggggggggggggggggggggggggggggggggggggggggggggg
hhhhhhhhhhhhhhhhhhhhhhhhhhhhhhhhhhhhhhhhhhhhhhhhhhhhhhhhhhhhhhhhhhhhhhhhhh
tttttttttttttttttttttttttttttttttttttttttttttttttttttttttttttttttttttttttt
ssssssssssssssssssssssssssssssssssssssssssssssssssssssssssssssssssssssssss
hhhhhhhhhhhhhhhhhhhhhhhhhhhhhhhhhhhhhhhhhhhhhhhhhhhhhhhhhhhhhhhhhhhhhhhhhh
iiiiiiiiiiiiiiiiiiiiiiiiiiiiiiiiiiiiiiiiiiiiiiiiiiiiiiiiiiiiiiiiiiiiiiiiii
gggggggggggggggggggggggggggggggggggggggggggggggggggggggggggggggggggggggggg
hhhhhhhhhhhhhhhhhhhhhhhhhhhhhhhhhhhhhhhhhhhhhhhhhhhhhhhhhhhhhhhhhhhhhhhhhh
llllllllllllllllllllllllllllllllllllllllllllllllllllllllllllllllllllllllll
iiiiiiiiiiiiiiiiiiiiiiiiiiiiiiiiiiiiiiiiiiiiiiiiiiiiiiiiiiiiiiiiiiiiiiiiii
gggggggggggggggggggggggggggggggggggggggggggggggggggggggggggggggggggggggggg
hhhhhhhhhhhhhhhhhhhhhhhhhhhhhhhhhhhhhhhhhhhhhhhhhhhhhhhhhhhhhhhhhhhhhhhhhh
tttttttttttttttttttttttttttttttttttttttttttttttttttttttttttttttttttttttttt
ssssssssssssssssssssssssssssssssssssssssssssssssssssssssssssssssssssssssss
```

Haiku (1)

She paused as
she was making
herself up.

                                       Absence is often
                                       more cause than
                                       effect.

The trick is getting
complimentary pens
to write.

indistinguishableindistinguishableindistinguishableindistingui
shableindistinguishableindistinguishableindistinguishableindi
stinguishableindistinguishableindistinguishableindistinguisha
bleindistinguishableindistinguishableindistinguishableindistin
guishableindistinguishableindistinguishableindistinguishablei
ndistinguishableindistinguishableindistinguishableindistinguis
hableindistinguishableindistinguishableindistinguishableindis
tinguishableindistinguishableindistinguishableindistinguishab
leindistinguishableindistinguishableindistinguishableindistingu
ishableindistinguishableindistinguishableindistinguishableind
distinguishableindistinguishableindistinguishableindistinguish
ableindistinguishableindistinguishableindistinguishableindisti
nguishableindistinguishableindistinguishableindistinguishable
indistinguishableindistinguishableindistinguishableindistingui
shableindistinguishableindistinguishableindistinguishableindi
stinguishableindistinguishableindistinguishableindistinguisha
bleindistinguishableindistinguishableindistinguishableindistin
guishableindistinguishableindistinguishableindistinguishablei
ndistinguishableindistinguishableindistinguishableindistinguis
hableindistinguishableindistinguishableindistinguishableindis
tinguishableindistinguishableindistinguishableindistinguishab
leindistinguishableindistinguishableindistinguishableindistingu
ishableindistinguishableindistinguishableindistinguishableind
distinguishableindistinguishableindistinguishableindistinguish
ableindistinguishableindistinguishableindistinguishableindisti
nguishableindistinguishableindistinguishableindistinguishable
indistinguishableindistinguishableindistinguishableindistingui
shableindistinguishableindistinguishableindistinguishableindi

Bee on Arrival

The day we came
up the steep stairs from the street
and then those
to the door

I noticed the lovely ochre
on the weatherboards
and the brass combination lock
on the door

and, as my eye lingered
over the long-stalked iceberg roses,
some touching the gloss-white picket fence,
while I listened to instructions over the intercom,
from a landlady, not far away,
about how to enter the code,

I saw a huge bee,
like no other I've ever seen,
ungainly as a lump of tar,
yet very endearing
as it hovered among
the white petals.
I thought it might be
a bumblebee.

Gardening

near where
my old dog lies
and where he sometimes
left his bones
I can't tell which
are his
or him.

STOP STOP STOP STOP START STOP

END OF THE LINE STOP START STOP STOP STOP STOP

A Detective Calls

Having examined the scene of the crime,
he attempts to expose
concealed items
in each suspect's heart and head

to the magnifying glass of questions
no more substantial than a
friction of air.

Language is the trap
he baits and sets
to tempt each into
a transparent lie

or that flickering
in eye or cheek
which, like an aftershock,
echoes the fatal act

when a slip of passion
pierced a heart
and splashed walls as white as clouds
in a stream of blood.

'MANIAR'

It's the largest city square in Europe,
the guide book says.

We sit down.

Lurid posters
(mostly flame and shadow)
advertise a feature on
the Bali bombing.

You take the thermos out and,
as we choose pastries,
a beggar
approaches.

'Maniar.
Maniar,'

he keeps on
saying.

He won't
go away.

Our last
tea-bag
falls
to the ground.

foreign

don't

let yourself go

they used to say

fairly sure about where

we came from

then

Conversations

on the way to funerals
even just about
where and when

quiet conversations
more gentle
than usual

The Detective

Himself the aftermath of murders
the detective scans the room.
Nothing is left out—
a cup on its side;
a pen on the floor;

an open book
and where
odd pages were
dog-eared.

To one whose life is bound
to the pursuit of crime
(and to his fans)
everything in
this room
(as in his world)

is obliged
to make sense
and take its place
in the items of evidence.

Gaps in meaning are where
murderers
creep through
with the certainty
of a revolver.

Loop: At The Kaiservilla

The leather chair still retains
his body's shape
and his last long hunting sock
is as yet unworn. The War came
and he never came back

and his wife's white wedding handkerchief
still rests on the pillow her head bled on
after the fatal stabbing

and every object, every picture
here proclaims
he's dead, she's dead, the son's dead,
even the nephew

they're all dead
it's
over.

life

Haiku (2)

                                        It looks like nothing
                                        she said and so I
                                        looked again.

a line too fine to be seen
disappearing
as you cross it

                                        just when you thought
                                        it was the last
                                        stair

TV People

A lot of people on TV are dead.
The old movies, documentaries
of the Royal Family, Hitler's Europe
—how many of the faces
breathe now?

Yet how real
they seem,
in colour or
in black and white

even when we know
the 'life' we're watching
was taped hours, days, years before

and that they
might be watching it,
comparing what they were
with how they seem.

It's as if the screen contains
a parallel universe, a dead star
off-loading its remains

providing 'company'
for those who understand
its comforts
and its limits.

Slips of the Tongue

In the cautious Fifties
Poirot was most himself
though soon to be
marooned
in time.

With all the talk of nuclear war,
hints of poison
at the vicar's tea-party
must've seemed
obscurely comforting

the menace and camaraderie
binding reader and detective
mirroring Cold War parades
with Eisenhower
saluting the boys

no one questioning
readers needing to lose themselves
in clues and lies
in narratives

where a false move
or slip of the tongue
might end the game
separating murderer forever
from hero and reader

in books dispersed now
on jumbled tables
at fêtes and op shops
selling cheap in faded covers

from which grey
detective faces
peer up

guarded
and estranged.

'Hanged'

We say a man is 'hanged'

because, while 'hung'
might

simplify the grammar,

it lacks the weight

of act and

intention.

Lost in the Emporium

I'm at the wrong exit.
I *thought* I was going the right way but
here are the stairs
to the wrong street.

I turn around. I go back.
I pass an information island.
There are two signs that say
CONCIERGE
but no one is there.

I look for signs that
I'm on the right track
but here's the *same* set of stairs
to the wrong street...

I *thought* I was travelling
in a straight line
but lines must *bend* in
an emporium.

I turn right and right again
I go on
but perhaps the exits have changed
or the shops around them...

But the street,
the *street* can't change.

Am I losing my way
or losing my mind?
I turn around again. I go back...

But what does it mean
'to go back'?
Can I
go back,
back where I came from
before entering the emporium?

no need

to fuss

the crows

will tidy up

when

we're gone

Haiku (3)

HISTORY
It all seemed to
happen very quickly
over a long time.

the local blues sounds
American, the voice of America
always in our ears

ODD
the noting of 'his'
in 'history' but not
'rapist' in 'therapist'

When the first knight
appeared

brilliant
in his perfect
shell

each detail
the work of
dreams

'They'll never
kill him!'

they
screamed.

Homage to the Arts of Empire

Watching riot police,
shield to shield,
on the other side of a bridge
in Grenoble I sensed
how overwhelming are
the arts of empire.

Not a demonstrator,
I'd time to admire
all that black
each detail caught
in the camera's lens
jaw-strap
and chin pad.

Could the designers
have gone too far?
Were the gloves and boots
real leather?

Too true to the classics perhaps
with motifs referencing
storm troopers of the
imagination
Gestapo, Star Wars, even
ancient Greek vases with their
silhouette-warriors

and somehow, subliminally
the Marseillaise
ringing out for Napoleon
or anyone else in love
with near-art-perfect
boots and tunics!

How could about-to-be-downtrodden
protesters confronting such
gorgeous, gleaming, long batons
not be overwhelmed by
the triumph of art?

The Joker exclaiming
in a Batman film somewhere:

Where
does he get
those wonderful toys?

Celebration Day

our normal lives/ a community day/watching the march/
security checks/a pleasant face/revellers/fireworks/people
like yourselves/if you see something/not quite right/bollards/
bollards/standing by/security guards/orderly fashion/fellow
Australians/extreme measures/CBE lockdown/counter-
terror/large trucks in place/risk assessment/vehicle
mitigation/bollards/bollards/high visibility/ alcohol-fuelled/
scanning barrier/ bollards/ bollards/security plan/breath
tests/semi-automatic weapons/vehicle-born terror /security
wands/persons of interest/persons of interest/helping
police/with investigations/breath/tests/breath/tests

Appearances

In some old paintings
children appear
as adults

stiffly standing
in curious versions
of their parents'
clothes

small faces displaying
the authority
of wealth.

Afterwards

generally earlier
than you'd like
it's time to un-
decorate
the tree

put glass balls in
padded cells

dump
the dead thing
outside
the back door

wondering how
to get rid of it.

No one sits down in our street.
They've removed the seats
because no one
sits down in our street.

*just as the radio guru
began to say what I had to do
the kettle came on the boil
and I couldn't hear*

Dracula Comes Home

As page after page
in Bram Stoker's novel
knitted together his flesh, clothes,
nature and history, Dracula
entered the imagination
of the late Nineteenth Century

since then
reappearing in different forms,
sometimes as woman, dog or Negro
but more often as
his old self

though set in
different periods
and portrayed in
different media

till it seems that soon
he'll be
everywhere,
not just when a bat is seen
across the moon
but wherever
libraries and video shops
stock creatures like him
for the mind
to feed on.

Finishing Stroke   *Peter Murphy*

He seems to be
very much at home
in our time
and to be settling in,
more and more,
as time goes on

just as we're growing
ever more appreciative
of his company.
We have the affinity
of blood relations

and it seems we're
very much
to his liking
and that he too
has something
we desire.

SOMETHING

in our imagination
attaches claws to the
feet of tables.

Finishing Stroke   Peter Murphy

Haiku (4)

        eternal
        'sleep
        mode'

minimalist
master-
pieces

                always
                just one
                slipper

Behind the Window

In afternoons at my grandaunt's place
as she sat in the dining room
with the mantelpiece
with the big mirror

I'd go into the small backyard
with the thick couch grass
to stare through the window
of a room I never entered

at pieces of furniture
piled on top of each other
as far as I could see.

CLOUD OF FORGETFULNESS #3

Virtual Germany

On my only day in Germany
nearly thirty years ago, I saw no traces
of the Second World War in what I thought of
as the present.

Now even the Nightwatchman
in Rothenburg boasts that only sixty per cent
of his town was bombed, and churches
have permanent exhibitions
devoted to their damages and when and how
repairs were carried out

and saints that seem fading to ghosts
appear as post-war reconstructions
in the notes.

Why are the remains of the past, even
Hitler's amphitheatres,
being revitalised
in the light of
memories and photographs?

Who's looking for what in these
reconstituted
ashes?

Who *is* George Clooney?

I've seen him in coffee ads
but why *him*?

I haven't seen him in films
or if I have, I can't remember.
I heard he had a villa
at Lake Como but he sold it.
I've heard of places where he's been
even seen a restaurant where he's been seen
but only seen him in ads.

He was at the big wedding
but who was he with?
He's been seen with politicians
but what did they say?
People who've met him
say he calls them John.

But what does he *do*
when he's not being seen?
Does he sleep at night?
Does he have bad dreams?
Does he pay his bills?
Does he wash his hands?

Does he wonder what to do today
and why everyone wants to see him?
Just who *is* George Clooney
and where does he come from?

People Begging

in this country we're
visiting

don't look at us
too closely

or ask
for much.

We give
a little

and leave them to
whatever.

Correction

They've removed the bushes that used to conceal
what, if anything, was happening behind them
so the question that was never officially asked
no longer needs an answer.

*somewhere
in the growth of science
and the history of toilets
the night soil man
disappears*

Finishing Stroke   Peter Murphy

the machine jars
as I turn the switch
and the year and its documents
begin to shred

Movie

In an early Twentieth Century film
a young boy walks quickly
keeping pace with the camera
to stay in the picture
as long as he can.

*It's the faces in the background
that say so much more
when the famous
politician is speaking.*

The Albums

Decades after the event
I buy the albums.
There are all these envelopes of
photographs
and sleeves of negatives

but who
are these people?

SUUBLIME

Icon

one of our icons
the bombed-out car
in the paddock
completely rusted

sometimes
with a door
missing

and always
at the back
of the mind

questions about
when
and how
and

why

Sedative Ad

Beneath a night sky
the river crosses the graphic plain.
The grass on the banks,
at the bottom of the picture,
is dark green.

The moon, unseen above,
is enlarged on the water
and underlined in ripples.
That this spells danger
can be seen in the woman's stance
as she sits by the bank
to right of centre.

Her white dress is intensified
by moonlight,
her heel tucked beneath her thigh
so daintily the viewer doesn't notice
immediately
her head's too low.

Her blonde hair
and the careless grip
on her large straw hat
make the hint of suicide
more appealing than compelling

as neat words, superimposed
upon the grass, urge:
'If you feel the patient is quite safe
without medication,
your choice
of another form of therapy
may be realistic.'

The brand name floats
across the sky and,
in a corner of the page,
below an asterisk,

a box of fine white print
is tucked
away.

The Tourist's Fear of Missing Something

We've followed the guidebook's
recommendations
checked every brochure
but still
a doubt remains...

Was there a sight
worth all the others

and we missed it?

Autopsy Shows

The suspect is interrogated endlessly.
Viewers can't get enough.
The mouth, the soul's canal,
is pumped for truth,
the psyche beaten on all sides,
till the precious flow begins.

Viewers *must* be satisfied. Therefore,
because mouths must stop at last
and insubstantial words must fail,
corpses on hard operating tables
are defiled by questions
and the contents of dead bellies
methodically exposed
to forensic tests

till truth comes out
of the remains of characters we knew
(some, half under sheets, still open to our gaze)
and in the relentless sifting of clues
in the cells of the deceased
(fingernails no less than seminal fluid)
the spirit ultimately appears
as a fiction of the flesh.

Goodbye Tiny Tim

Tiny Tim
is gone

voice
pitch
ukulele

no
'tiptoe
through the
tulips'

no
broken /
unbroken
voice

no

tiny

tim.

Running Back

He has to be the last one out
of his mind. His house, their house
moments from shattering into fire
as he's seen the others further out.
As yet intact, its frame still nets items trapped from the years,
objects which are memories—beds, shoes, shirts: it's a mesh which is
himself; wife; children—even more than him,
the sediment of his time. He's heard so many minds burn
this week; seen so many houses
flashing over time, sinking into their shadows, ash,
unlike flesh which spills from its frame. He can't let his
'self' vanish. Tossing out what time is left, he still hangs on
more scared by that drop into a life without remembering
than blasting off with doors and windows shut.
But there's that other 'house' (there has to be)… one that mustn't go
when everything in his brain is fire
—now the hose is useless, its last drop steam
on the skin of his cocoon—
his photograph album.
The prospect of those 'moments', snaps,
cards which have played him out, bending into dust
—dark spots in a chest of fire—is too much for him, as,
thinking about escape, he's turned around,
into a span of time he can't elude…
still groping for his eyes, his book of dreams,
held fast in nothing but transparencies…
now it's all, along with him
blowing
away.

101 Dalmatians

Decades after the Second World War
the long marches across the globe
by armies and prisoners of war
must've made an impression on
the Disney Studios.

Chased by the vicious Cruella De Vil,
convoys of puppies race across snow and ice
spattering the wastes with shadowy dots
and gliding down
frozen rivers

guided by careful leaders
who count them off with patient smiles
as they trip or fall over checkpoints.

A hundred and
one…

each angling its tiny face
as they make the same
leap of trust across misty space

making their way
home.

Haiku (5)

Silence doesn't 'come'.
Rather, something ends or
doesn't start.

                the sincerest admiration…
                a plagiarist stealing
                your mind

                          As the word 'hope'
                          came into my mind
                          instinctively I looked behind.

Always Eating

The article is about where to
go
for the best
cappuccino

and there's a large
photo
of a massive
cup

with a cloud of froth
and magnified
chocolate
dust.

You can never
have

too
much.

Bench

This is my father's work bench
his last metal filings
flecked in the surface
wood dust too.

He had a more definite idea
about what he was doing here

it seems to me
as I file a chip
to plug a gap
and my dust falls
on his.

Finishing Stroke　　　　　　　　　　　　　　　　Peter Murphy

I remember her last call
from hospital
saying she didn't want
to go on living
but didn't think
of calling back:
it seemed a
random call
her last
to me.

Entering

I cross the beam of the security light,
observing how far darkness
is pushed back,
and, climbing the stairs, turn the key
in the deadlock

and, as the door swings open, hear an
intermittent beep warning
the alarm is armed

and, in the sixty-second delay,
punch in the code,

then remove the key
and shut the door.

minimuminimuminimuminimuminimuminimuminimuminimumin
imuminimuminimuminimuminimuminimuminimuminimuminimu
minimuminimuminimuminimuminimuminimuminimuminimumin
imuminimuminimuminimuminimuminimuminimuminimuminimu
minimuminimuminimuminimuminimuminimuminimuminimumin
imuminimuminimuminimuminimuminimuminimuminimuminimu
minimuminimuminimuminimuminimuminimuminimuminimumin
imuminimuminimuminimuminimuminimuminimuminimuminimu
minimuminimuminimuminimuminimuminimuminimuminimumin
imuminimuminimuminimuminimuminimuminimuminimuminimu
minimuminimuminimuminimuminimuminimuminimuminimumin
imuminimuminimuminimuminimuminimuminimuminimuminimu
minimuminimuminimuminimuminimuminimuminimuminimumin
imuminimuminimuminimuminimuminimuminimuminimuminimu
minimuminimuminimuminimuminimuminimuminimuminimumin
imuminimuminimuminimuminimuminimuminimuminimuminimu
minimuminimuminimuminimuminimuminimuminimuminimumin
imuminimuminimuminimuminimuminimuminimuminimuminimu
minimuminimuminimuminimuminimuminimuminimuminimumin
imuminimuminimuminimuminimuminimuminimuminimuminimu
minimuminimuminimuminimuminimuminimuminimuminimumin
imuminimuminimuminimuminimuminimuminimuminimuminimu
minimuminimuminimuminimuminimuminimuminimuminimumin
imuminimuminimuminimuminimuminimuminimuminimuminimu
minimuminimuminimuminimuminimuminimuminimuminimumin

Fox

Yesterday a fox came into our garden
when I was turning off the alarm.

It saw me through the window
as I saw it flex, alert,
waiting perhaps,
for a move on my part

or a shift in its programming
that would take it away so quickly
I scarcely remember its going

and in my mind it's still there
flexed, alert, beautiful
and threatening…

or was it
a cat?

Finishing Stroke   *Peter Murphy*

Whether across the sky
or over the road
I always just miss
the shape of bat
the colour of fox.

Wings of Angels

At funerals I watch the
wings of angels
progress across
the roofs of churches.

Spread or furled, they
suggest no link
with flight or flapping

as angels
hang around the sky
in a physical dispensation
from disbelief

never tucking in
those wings
to almost nothing
as birds can.

The Blank Page

measures
you

what you can bear
to see in print and

what you'd like
to be seen as yours

and as words
cross pages

what you never
write

shouts
from the margins.

Haiku (6)

At the wedding a voice
from the back. "It shoulda been
ME!"

                    WELCOME!

                    ENTER

                    AT OWN RISK.

                                            KEEP DOOR SHUT
                                            it says, but it isn't
                                            so...

Grand Prix

Though a long way from the
Colosseum

in which a red wave would cross
the field of play

till it spilled through ducts
leading underground

making pools in bull rings
in later centuries
miniscule

this place connects with it
through skill and

the chance
of death.

Cursor

As the pen slides across the page
pause in mid-
thought

and watch the first half
gestate to
scribbled words
as the second
dissipates between your ears.

Call it back
but will it come
it or a mate,
and will you know?

Or,
scarcely looking at
the cursor

I-
ing on
your computer screen,

fill blinking space
with letter after letter,
but with whose
words,

whose
I?

What becomes of the Queen's hats?

After each spectacular event?
Do gloved hands reverently
rest each one

on a gilt-edged shelf
in the Royal
Archive?

Or are they buried deep
in the Royal Crypt
where she eventually
will join them

or are they taken apart
by the Royal Milliner
after dark
and secretly resewn
so they seem like new
to the untrained eye

and what becomes
of Putin's dogs
and Trump's Towers

and where
where
are Imelda's shoes?

That Face

The strategies of power
are more or less
the same. After seeking to keep his
face
hidden from the press
Hitler discovered a photographer
capable of imagining him
as he wished to be seen

subsequently having
all other images
annihilated

and anyone who thinks
it's different in our
Commonwealth should try
publishing a photo of the Queen
without the Palace's
Approval.

Europe and Almonds

Still remembering an odour
rich with almonds
on a morning
in Amsterdam
(long after I'd been excited
by existentialism)

I'd like to celebrate what
Europe's done with almonds

especially those
achievements with almond meal
in all kinds of casing –
pastry, cake, bread,
confectionery.

Of course, there's nothing wrong
with almonds as almonds
but invention changes
landscapes

changed my mind
when a tree root in *Nausea*
horrified
a narrator.

Haiku (7)

mid-afternoon
lights in every house
coronavirus

                                      hard to imagine stones getting through
                                      the tiny gaps between
                                      sock and shoe

                                                                               every
                                                                               bubble
                                                                               bursts

Bodies on TV

At first there wasn't any apprehension
when the tellies moved in.
What could they do
that radio hadn't?

There was the evening news, of course,
and the chance that pictures
might hurt more than words

but no one wanted to offend
and news merged easily with films
musicals and soaps

till somewhere around Vietnam
when Westerns seemed almost dead
real
bodies began to appear
on black and white
screens...
melting, blackening, flaring
with napalm

and a kneeling Vietnamese,
hands tied behind the back,
was shot in the head
in every lounge.

After that the medium
couldn't go back,

though the flesh comes now
from other wars, famines,
one-off atrocities
and the road toll

whereas radio
settled for talk shows,
the Top 40,
gardening
and nostalgia.

Powerful Friends

In churches over Easter
music calls upon
the ultimate
being

suggesting a desire for
that all-powerful 'friend'
such as Australia is
forever
trying to find

found once in England
still finds in America
while glancing uneasily
towards China.

'FREE DUBCEK'

Looking at photos of tanks
moving into the Prague Spring
a middle-aged Scot recalls seeing
'FREE DUBCEK' on a Glasgow wall
after 'Communism with a Human Face'
had brought the Russians in.

Though the Council erased the words
they were to appear again and again
achieving no more
than those who died in front of tanks

and cries of protest still go up
grandmas still join the ranks
confused kids wheel prams among the chaos
few of the protestors expecting
an order to fire
with them in mind

so many cries of anger, tears, messages
on walls or over bitumen
like one on a Roman footpath
calling for the release of
Piccolo Tommaso

kidnapped at seventeen months
and killed in twenty minutes because
he wouldn't stop
crying.

Friday Night in the Supermarket

It seems neater than normal
as if there's been an
extra clean-up
for the weekend.

Though nothing's obviously different
an almost palpable buzz
moves through the place.

Staff chat about
what they're going
to do.

There's a glassy look
in the checkout chick's eyes.

Even the Cool Section's
clear plastic flaps'
fut-fut

echoes
that unspoken thought:

escape.

Boredom

Wanting to do
something

to be/
have...

other than...

The cup
sits on the plate.

The window is neither
open nor closed

and through a small space
as yet unsealed

a silent draught
crosses the room.

Gerry's Bag

It's forty years
since that end of term

the first
in my second job

my bag
packed for Mt Buffalo
under my desk

unlike Gerry's
near-new
kit-bag
square in the centre
of his empty desk
his almost neat hat
nearby

as he sat in anticipation
in his gaberdine coat
discussing the crossword
with Merv behind

both waiting
for the time
to go.

Desktop Diary

I've worked in places rich in bulldog clips
and gliding clips and reams of A4 paper
(even lined foolscap!)
and biros and typewriters and
rulers and envelopes and bins and
pencils and erasers and staplers
and in-trays and out-trays and clip-boards
and adjustable chairs and lockers
and desks and drawers

and where on every desk
the first page for the start of each day
was on a desktop diary pierced
by holes through which rings
held it all in place
where the first thought to reach
each employee's brain
was the daily quote at the foot of the page

though the only one that comes to me now
is 'The man who trusts no one knows
he himself is
not to be trusted.'

Haiku (8)

Sliding back the peephole guard
she fears appearing in
another's gaze.

a train whistle
crossing
centuries

Jottings in the Margin

When I heard someone complain
about a reader who'd underlined '<u>death</u>'
whenever it appeared

I wondered what others made
of those brief texts I'd scribbled in the margins,
always intending to erase.

Since then I've come to appreciate
the commentaries that others leave
outside the print

sometimes checking their impressions
against my own
(readers mumbling
behind an author's back)

or enjoying the marginal relevance
of students' disgust
at set texts…

though never once
encountering
the '<u>death</u>'-
underliner.

There's something about the suburbs
when relative silence comes with lights
and night-walkers monitoring
their heart-rates.

The owner walks the dog
in one hand a leash
in the other
a plastic bag.

Venice

On Wednesday nights
I pass a house called
'Venice'.

From down the road
an amber streak says
someone's there and may be
watching.
It's the porch lighting
which spills onto
a postcard garden.

Along the path
which curves to the gate
rose bushes are in silhouette,
small shapes picked out
in primary colours
and black.
The lawn is a shallow pool
of green.

On either side of the door
windows glow
(drapes tied
with a bow)
though what's inside
remains
obscured.

The porch is both
in shadows and
illuminated,
and over the many
glass panels in the
door,

VENICE

—in large thick letters,
gently curved—

beats
          like a heart.

ANTARCTICA

FAR
FAR
UNDER COLD STARS
COLD COLD
ANTARCTICA
MELTS MELTS MELTS
FAR
FAR
UNDER WHITE STARS
COLD COLD
ANTARCTICA
MELTS MELTS MELTS
FAR FAR
UNDER DARK SKIES
COLD WHITE
ANTARCTICA
MELTS MELTS MELTS
ON BLACK SEAS
UNSEEN
UNSEEN
FAR
FAR
COLD COLD
ANTARCTICA
IS MELTING MELTING
MELTING

Haiku (9)

                in the blink of an eye
                the click of a mouse the
                undetectable lie

                                        Sometimes I think I have
                                        a liar's feeling
                                        for the truth.

Green

Never far
from bus or train
SHERWOOD appears

in local signs
for street or park,
forest even.

Once, besotted with
the Hollywood film,
Melbourne thought often
of the Green Man.

Because celluloid preserves flesh
we can watch dead actors
fall in love on digital screens.

TERMS AND CONDITIONS

Don't think about it.*
Don't think about it.*
Don't think about it.*
Don't think about it.*
Don't think about it.*
Don't think about it.*
Don't think about it.*
Don't think about it.*
Don't think about it.*
Don't think about it.*
Don't think about it.*
Don't think about it.*
Don't think about it.*
Don't think about it.*
Don't think about it.*
Don't think about it.*
Don't think about it.*
Don't think about it.*
Don't think about it.*
Don't think about it.*
Don't think about it.*
Don't think about it.*
Don't think about it.*

ACCEPT

* blah blah blah blah blah blah blah blah blah
blah blah blah blah blah blah blah blah blah
blah blah blah blah blah blah blah blah blah
blah blah blah blah blah blah blah blah blah

an old handmower
stem painted deep blue
wheels totally rusted
rests against a lemon tree
in overgrown grass

dead over fifty years
my old dog's bones
still follow me
round the garden

after a long sermon
on what we can learn
from a dog's need for love
he went home to spend
the day with his cat

Peoples permanently at war

need
to celebrate it.

You see children climbing over tanks
in films about the Third Reich
perhaps feeling powerful
and loved up there.

And songs are important too
though as the Empire began to fail
the lyrics switched

from victory
to glorious death.

plus

−

minus

The Right Notes

Not surprisingly
those who supply notes
for electronic organs

record
real ones played on
real organs

and include the sound of stops
and other incidental
distractions.

What can you edit out
without losing
everything?

For the slow

person the time... time
has already passed—

no need to think
about what
to do.

What to do Next

Get up and walk around.
Yawn. Think.
Look at what's in your pocket.
Check off a list.

Yawn again.
Stretch.
Sit up straight.
Slouch.
Deal with anxieties.
Relax.

Remember who you are.
Attempt to solve problems.
Reflect on your future.

Put your right leg
over your left
till it feels
uncomfortable,

then your left
over your right.
Sit up straight.
Pause.

Try to think…
Try not
to think…

Pause…

Person or Persons Unknown

There's a remark about
'small Latin and less Greek'
undercut by doubt about
the mood of the verb

no one at the time
having said a word
in clarification

and apart from that and being called
an 'upstart crow' no one seems
to have said anything
least of all him.

It's believed he died of a fever
after a night at the pub
but no one has said
what he said that night
or on any other

and after all the performances
of all those plays
(and he acted in some)

there's no record
of what he said
about any of them
if he said anything.

Finishing Stroke   *Peter Murphy*

Most famous of all
his contemporaries
he slipped through history
like a thief through a crowd

no one apparently
having seen
or heard
anything.

Not surprisingly some think
he was someone else
but which one... ?

FOOTNOTES

underneath the normal text
in a history book
endless footnotes – in tiny font – confronted me

addressing matters barely touched on
in the giant three or four lines above

fragments of information
difficult to connect
with anything

Finishing Stroke   Peter Murphy

                                                       in

                                                       the

                                                      full
                                                         ness

                                                       of

                                                   time

                                                         space

                                                             emp
                                                                 ties

2 0 22 *

*Where do you place the Doomsday hand?

About the Author

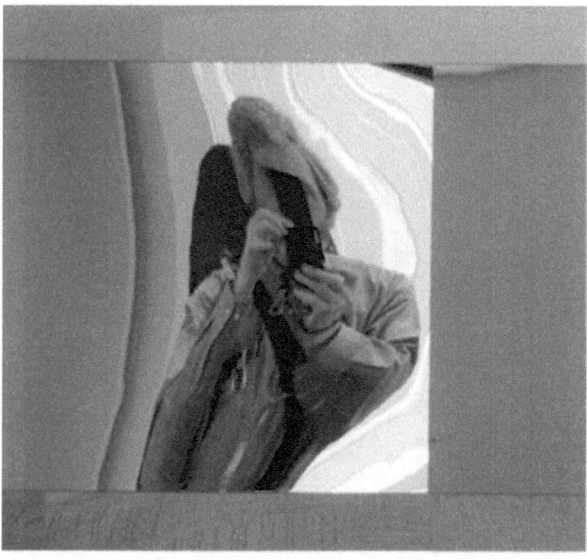

Born in Melbourne in 1945, the day before Hiroshima, I began writing in the middle 1960s, first poetry, later short stories, still later plays and novels. I've always liked Wittgenstein's idea that the purpose of philosophy is to enable the fly to get out of the fly-bottle and, in my work, across a range of writing forms, art and photography, I examine different ways of seeing and considering the world. I look for the 'whole' of life in everyday things, events and shared culture. My approach is low-key and indirect, looking at what a hole might tell us about a rabbit. Also, in exploring all this, I keep brushing against my own consciousness of mortality—and there's a sense of grace or elegance or just neatness in things, even in our own absurdities.

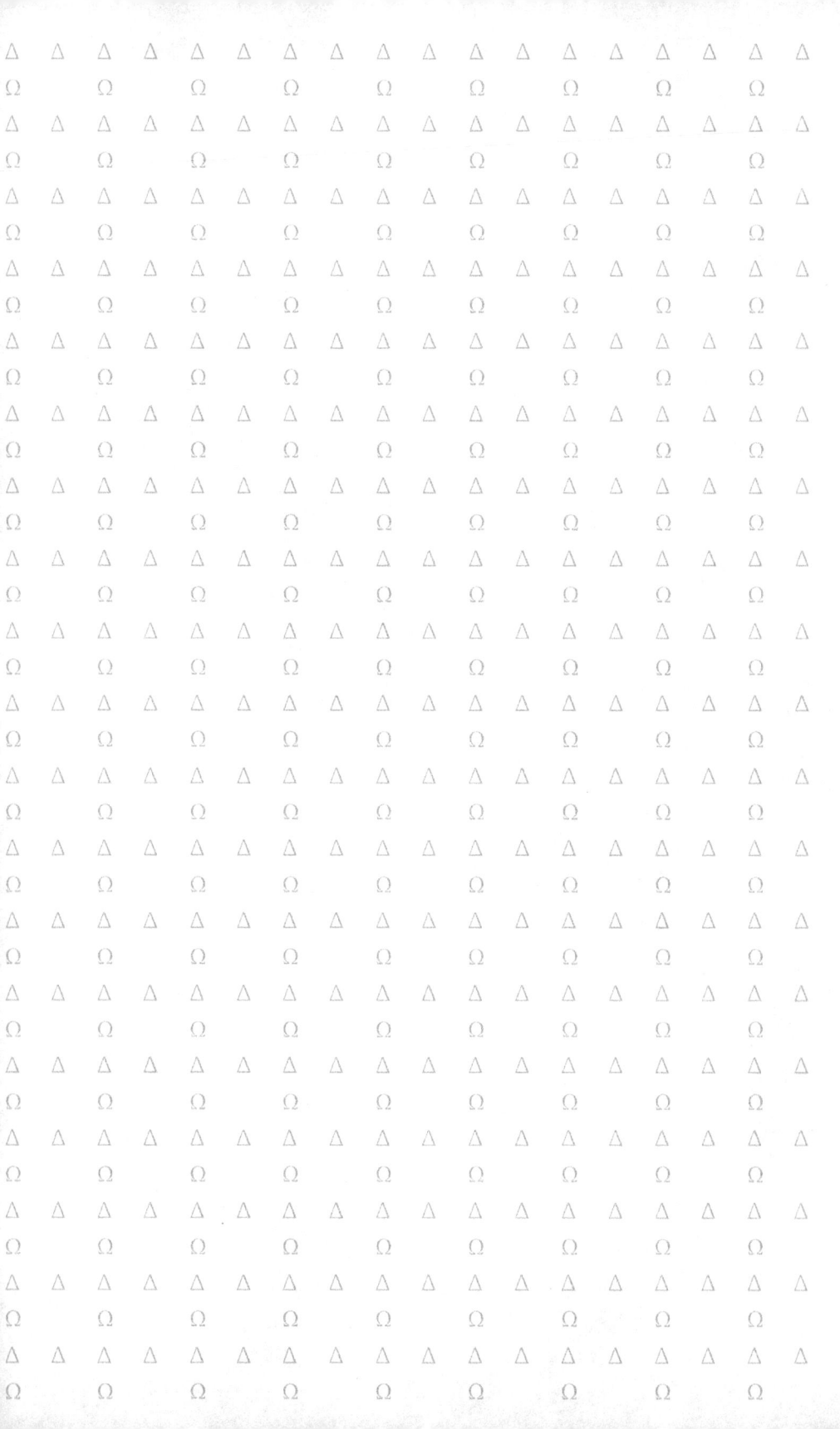

www.ingramcontent.com/pod-product-compliance
Lightning Source LLC
Chambersburg PA
CBHW022018290426
44109CB00015B/1214